Animals on the Farm

Pigs

Linda Aspen-Baxter
and Heather Kissock

MEDIA ENHANCED BOOKS
AV2 BY WEIGL
ADDED VALUE • AUDIO VISUAL

www.av2books.com

Go to **www.av2books.com**, and enter this book's unique code.

BOOK CODE

Q 3 6 3 4 9 6

AV² by Weigl brings you media enhanced books that support active learning.

AV² provides enriched content that supplements and complements this book. Weigl's AV² books strive to create inspired learning and engage young minds in a total learning experience.

Your AV² Media Enhanced books come alive with...

Audio
Listen to sections of the book read aloud.

Video
Watch informative video clips.

Embedded Weblinks
Gain additional information for research.

Try This!
Complete activities and hands-on experiments.

Key Words
Study vocabulary, and complete a matching word activity.

Quizzes
Test your knowledge.

Slide Show
View images and captions, and prepare a presentation.

... and much, much more!

Published by AV² by Weigl
350 5ᵗʰ Avenue, 59ᵗʰ Floor
New York, NY 10118
Website: www.av2books.com   www.weigl.com

Library of Congress Cataloging-in-Publication Data

Kissock, Heather.
 Pigs / Heather Kissock and Linda Aspen-Baxter.
   p. cm. -- (Animals on the farm)
 ISBN 978-1-61690-928-4 (hardcover : alk. paper) -- ISBN 978-1-61690-574-3 (online)
1. Swine--Juvenile literature. I. Aspen-Baxter, Linda. II. Title.
 SF395.5.K576 2011
 636.4--dc23
                            2011023413

Printed in the United States of America in North Mankato, Minnesota
1 2 3 4 5 6 7 8 9 0   15 14 13 12 11

062011
WEP030611

Senior Editor: Heather Kissock   Art Director: Terry Paulhus

Weigl acknowledges Getty Images as the primary image supplier for this title.

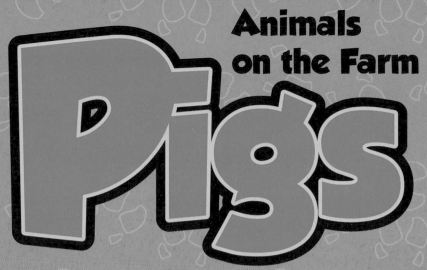

Animals on the Farm
Pigs

CONTENTS

2   AV² Book Code
4   Why Farmers Keep Me
6   What Kind of Animal I Am
8   How I Move
10 More About Me
12 What I Eat
14 How I Talk
16 Being With Others
18 Having Babies
20 My Babies
22 Pig Facts
24 Word List

4

I am a large farm animal.
Farmers keep me for my meat.

5

I am a mammal. My body
is covered with hair.

I have four sturdy legs that help me move around. Each leg has four toes at the bottom.

9

I have a long snout with a flat end. It lets me smell everything around me.

11

I eat both plants and meat. Farmers often give me grains to eat.

13

**How do I talk to other pigs?
I grunt and squeal.**

I like to be with other pigs. We have fun running and rolling around.

I give birth to babies
up to three times each year.

My babies are called piglets.

My babies are very small at first. I make sure they are kept warm and safe.

PIG FACTS

This page provides more detail about the interesting facts found in the book. Simply look at the corresponding page number to match the fact.

Pages 4-5

Pigs are large farm animals. Farmers keep them for their meat. There are different sizes and types of pigs. Some pigs grow very large. Others are much smaller, or miniature. Pigs can be brown, black, white, or pink. There are about 90 pig breeds in total.

Pages 6–7

Pigs are mammals. Their bodies are covered with hair. Hair is just one of three main mammal features. Mammals are also warm-blooded. This means they are able to generate their own body heat. As well, the female of any mammal species is able to make milk to give to her young.

Pages 8–9

Pigs have four toes at the bottom of each leg. Each toe has a hoof, which protects the toe when the pig is moving around. Pigs only use the longer, middle toes when walking and running. The toes are pointed downward, so a pig actually tiptoes when it walks. The outer toes are used for balance and rarely touch the ground.

Pages 10–11

Pigs have a long snout with a flat end. The snout can move up and down, and from side to side. This allows the pig to smell everything around it. Pigs also use their snout to dig deep in the dirt for food. The snout is a pig's most sensitive body part. A pig's sense of smell is so strong that, in France, pigs are trained to dig up truffles.

Pages 12–13

Pigs eat both plants and meat. Farmers often give them grains, such as corn, barley, and oats, to eat. Pigs eat about 8 pounds (4 kilograms) of food each day. However, they will eat all day if food is available. Pigs are naturally lean animals. If a pig is fat, it is probably being overfed.

Pages 14–15

Pigs talk to each other by grunting and squealing. A mother pig grunts when she is feeding her young. Pigs also bark. This is usually done to warn other pigs of danger. Pigs squeal when they are about to be fed. They can also squeal when they are upset. A pig's squeal can be almost as loud as the engine of a jet airplane during takeoff.

Pages 16–17

Pigs like to be with other animals. They are social animals that live together in groups called herds. There can be two to eight pigs in a herd. Pigs like to spend their time running, rolling, and playing. Some pigs can run as fast as 11 miles (18 kilometers) per hour. Pigs enjoy swimming as well.

Pages 18–19

Pigs give birth to babies up to three times each year. Sows, or female pigs, carry their babies for about 115 days before giving birth. Piglets are always born in litters. This means many piglets are born at once. There are usually 8 to 12 piglets per litter. At birth, piglets are hairless and pink.

Pages 20–21

Piglets are very small at first. They weigh only about 2 to 4 pounds (1 to 2 kg). At this stage, piglets are very delicate and need to be kept warm. After one month, however, they are weaned, or removed from their mother's milk. They then begin to eat grains like other pigs. By 6 months of age, they weigh about 230 pounds (104 kg).

WORD LIST

Research has shown that as much as 65 percent of all written material published in English is made up of 300 words. These 300 words cannot be taught using pictures or learned by sounding them out. They must be recognized by sight. This book contains 51 common sight words to help young readers improve their reading fluency and comprehension. This book also teaches young readers several important content words, such as proper nouns. These words are paired with pictures to aid in learning and improve understanding.

Page	Sight Words First Appearance
5	a, animal, for, I, keep, large, me, my
6	is, with
8	around, at, each, four, has, have, help, me, move, that, the
11	a, end, it, lets, long
13	and, both, eat, give, often, to
15	do, how, other, talk
16	be, like, running, we
18	three, times, up, year
19	are, called
21	first, make, small, they, very

Page	Content Words First Appearance
5	farmers, meat
6	body, hair, mammal
8	bottom, legs, toes
11	snout
13	grains, meat, plants
15	pigs
18	babies, birth
19	piglets

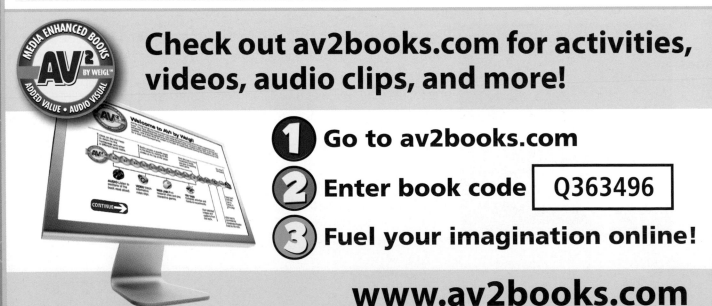

Check out av2books.com for activities, videos, audio clips, and more!

1 Go to av2books.com

2 Enter book code **Q363496**

3 Fuel your imagination online!

www.av2books.com